BACKYARD CHICKENS

Tips And Tricks For Healthy And Strong Chickens

Sam Norton

Sam Norton

Sam Norton

TABLE OF CONTENTS

Sam Norton

Introduction

Chickens are found all over the world in a variety of shapes and sizes. They easily adapt to new environments and offer a range of possibilities to their owners, from being kept as pets to becoming a steady source of income.

The reasons for chicken keeping are as diverse as the people who keep chickens. They certainly have more benefits than negatives in their keeping, and once you begin it will be hard to look back and not feel satisfied with your feathered backyard flock.

Why People Keep Chickens

Having an available daily stock of fresh eggs is something that many cooking enthusiasts can only dream of.

There is something about freshly laid eggs that is just unique. They taste better, last longer, and are way more nutritious for you.

Jenny McGruther (2018), a well-known food specialist and holistic nutritionist, has some interesting insights into why people should keep chickens.

In most counties across the U.S. there are certain laws to adhere to when keeping chickens and one of the most common is that the chickens should be hens and forbid the keeping of roosters.

The obvious three A.M. crowing may be one of the main reasons for this law. But hens are definitely more valuable in keeping, in any case, unless you specifically want chicks. So here are some of the main reasons to keep chickens (or hens):

Eggs

Fresh eggs are simply that. Fresh, they taste better, and given that you know just what your hens have been eating, you know exactly what you end up eating.

Since you can also be assured that they are laid in the natural time cycle (about one egg every 25 hours), you know that you will be getting quality and size. For those of us who love cooking or baking, this will be a blessing, as large eggs will be consistent for the most part.

In commercial chicken farming, most hens are kept in a battery system, where they are caged, have limited mobility (if any) and are fed sometimes questionable foods to increase the production of eggs.

At such battery farms, the lights are, for instance, set on a timer to fool the hens into thinking that two days have passed, instead of one, and as a result, they will then lay more than one egg every 25 hours.

There is also an increased awareness of the introduction of growth hormones and other chemicals to influence the color of commercially produced eggs.

If we are what we eat, then what will this end up doing to us? In the long run, having fresh eggs may not only be about taste, but also about health.

For a steady supply of eggs, you can calculate how many hens to keep, bearing in mind that not all your hens will necessarily begin laying at the same time.

If a hen lays an egg once a day, then you would keep six hens should you need half-dozen eggs daily. If you decide to keep a surplus of eggs, it is a good idea to write the lay-date on each egg that you store. But more on eggs later...

Healthier Food Sources

Many of us consume both eggs and chicken as a food source, and this may at times not be the healthiest option given that commercially kept chickens live in environments that are ill-suited to producing healthy animals.

Factory farms feed their chickens on corn, cottonseed, and soy—all grown as GMO (Genetically Modified Organism) crops. This means that the meat or eggs that you buy in a store may not be beneficial to your health.

Organically reared animals and free-range eggs are certainly healthier, yet products claiming to be GMO-free are at times suspect, as everything from the fertilizers used to the pest control policies of that particular farm, may influence the so-called natural state of its produce.

Raising your own chickens and using their eggs can offer you a real way to ensure that your family only gets the very best nutrition. Freshly laid organic eggs are quite expensive to buy at farmers' markets, but you can have your own hens produce equally delicious and nutritious eggs at a fraction of the cost; in fact, it will only cost you the price of your organically certified chicken pellets.

Leonard (2015) believes that backyard eggs contain more vitamin A and E, and Beta Carotene than battery eggs do, while free-range eggs contain 292mg Omega 3 versus only 0.033mg in battery eggs. These statistics certainly make free-range or backyard eggs a much better option than those tasteless battery eggs that you can buy at any local grocery store.

Teaching Your Family about Food

Anyone who has spent some time around kids will be able to attest to the fact that most children have no clue where their food comes from.

If you were to ask them where KFC comes from, they would say, "From the shop," and most of these kids would be absolutely surprised (and perhaps even a little disgusted) to know that chickens come from eggs, and that eggs are laid by hens.

If this is a life-view that persists, then it will be no surprise that children grow into adults who have no respect for or knowledge of food.

Keeping chickens allows for your family to build a deeper understanding of their role within the animal kingdom (yes, for all of our brainpower, we are still animals), and allow them to interact and influence the animals in their care.

You may see the utter surprise on your child's face the first time that they collect a freshly laid egg and realize that it is warm and still a little soft-shelled as it rests in their hands.

Being made responsible for feeding and cleaning after the chickens is also a great way to teach kids about responsibility and the fruits of their labor. Many farmers have taught their kids about food and responsible wealth management by letting them sell eggs raise chickens for slaughter, and understanding the basic principle of expenses versus income. By raising backyard chickens this is something that you can also do.

Chickens are omnivores and eat anything from the commercially available poultry feeds, maize crush, and garden bugs, to fruits and vegetables from your kitchen. Image: Arisa Chattasa on Unsplash.

Chickens are Convenient to Care for

After the initial time and money lay-out of getting chickens, building a safe area for them to move around in (or planning to let them free-range), and constructing a suitable coop, the actual time that they will require for maintenance is very little.

It takes less than ten minutes a day to water and feed them, and perhaps lock them up safely at night to ward off the prowling neighborhood cat. As a bonus, free-range chickens tend to fertilize your garden on their own, reducing the frequency with which you need to clean the coup area.

Feed wise, they require very little, and you can supplement their poultry pellets or maize crush with safe kitchen scraps, thereby helping with recycling natural waste materials from your home.

Most chicken feed is also relatively inexpensive when compared to dog food, for instance.

For the most part, your chickens will be quite happy to scratch away and eat whatever is available, and it's simply up to you to ensure that they have enough food and water available.

They eat all day long, so you don't have to keep mealtimes but don't be surprised if they do tend to hang around the kitchen door when you start cooking supper.

Bye-bye Bugs

Chickens are naturally happy to forage, and tasty bugs are a huge treat for them. They enjoy eating worms, beetles, crickets, larvae, slugs, spiders, and even scorpions (the small non-poisonous kinds).

A mother hen will put up quite a show as she teaches her chicks about catching and eating a worm for instance, and chickens supplement their diets by scratching throughout your garden to find tasty morsels. This is great news to any avid gardener, as their activities actually loosen the soil and keep unwanted pests at bay.

This will significantly cut down on your need to spray your yard with pesticides and since they poop naturally while scratching about, they even fertilize your yard for you. This brings us to the next point, fertilizer:

Chickens are Fertilizer Factories

Since chickens naturally scratch all around your yard in their daily foraging activities they also naturally poop and distribute that poop. Chicken poop is naturally rich in nitrogen and makes a great additive to your compost heap.

The only time that their poop needs to be managed, is when you let them roost naturally. In this case, you need to be prepared because they poop huge volumes at night while they sleep. So you may benefit from locking them in a coup at night not only to keep them safe, but also to manage where they poop, making it easier to clean up. Your neighbors might even come knocking on your door wanting some of their poop to give their lawns a dressing, since it is such an excellent fertilizer, and this again offers a potential for a small side business. If nothing else, it could partially pay for the chickens' feed.

Entertainment and Company

People also keep chickens not only as a source of income or due to them being an excellent food supply, but also because chickens are entertaining to watch and can even be quite sociable.

Chickens will naturally gather near you when you are chilling in the backyard, and they have loads of little antics that are entertaining to watch. Certainly, the mother hen with her brood of chicks sheltered under her wings is an endearing sight to behold. Hens have a little pecking order that they establish, and seeing them sort each other out can be quite entertaining.

Some chickens have a range of melodious sounds that they can produce, which are quite different from the loud clucking they make when they have laid an egg.

They can even produce a strange almost whistling sound in their throats that is quite lovely to hear. In colder weather, they huddle together for warmth, and don't be surprised if your braver hens decide to join you in the kitchen or snuggle up next to you on the back porch. Chickens make excellent pets too.

Chapter 1.
Tips and Trick on How to Choose the Correct Breed

Many chicken breeds are strikingly beautiful. However, if you rely on beauty alone as you choose birds for your flock, it can quickly lead to problems.

Each breed has its own unique characteristics. Factors like how large the birds are and their activity level play a major role in how much space they need.

Housing too many chickens in a small area can cause a high level of ammonia that is unhealthy and unsanitary—for you and your birds. Additionally, the male-to-female ratio should be considered as you think about size.

Below, we'll discuss some of the more common birds for backyards. Then we'll discuss a few of the rarer options, should you decide you want to collect chickens. Something to remember is that there is no one-size-fits-all description for these birds. All descriptions are generalized and each chicken will vary depending on its environment and upbringing. You should expect your chickens to have a unique personality that goes along with their breed description, though some birds have personalities far from what you are expecting from their descriptions.

Common Backyard Breeds

When you are beginning as a chicken farmer, it can be helpful to start with one of these more common backyard breeds. Most of these have been selected for their even temperament. They are easier to take care of than some other chicken breeds for this reason and you are less likely to have fighting among your birds.

Ameracauna Chickens

True Ameracauna chicks are known for their ability to lay blue eggs. However, they are a rare breed native to South America. In North America, the birds referred to as Ameracauna chickens or "Easter Eggers" are descendants of hens from Chile. They migrated to America in the 1970s.

The Ameracauna variety is a good choice for egg laying. They have exuberant personalities and lay pretty eggs in various shades of green, blue, and cream.

Leghorn Chickens

If you have a large flock, Leghorn chickens may not be a good choice. They are a good starter bird, but they startle easily and generally do not have calm personalities. People that do choose these chickens often choose them for their egg-laying, as they lay around 280 white eggs each year. Leghorn chickens are ideal for warmer climates.

Orpington Chickens

Buffs are the most common Orpington variety of chickens. They are usually gentle-natured birds with big, fluffy features. Orpington chickens serve two purposes. Even though they were originally bred for meat, they tolerate cold climates well and lay eggs through the winter, making them a great dual-purpose bird.

Families with young children may also appreciate these gentle birds as pets. They tolerate handling well and allow themselves to be picked up. As they are more docile birds, they are easier targets for predators. You will generally want to keep these birds in a fenced-in area to keep them safe.

Star Chickens

This variety is not formally recognized as a breed, but they are a common hybrid chicken. Varieties include the RedStar and BlackStar chickens.

One major benefit of this bird is the distinct difference in the coloring between male and female chicks, which is good if you are trying to keep the number of roosters on your farm balanced to the number of females.

The calm personality of Star chickens makes them a good choice for new bird farmers. They are also productive, laying about 260 brown eggs annually.

Sussex Chickens

Sussex chickens are another popular choice for families. They have curious and friendly personalities that make them very pet-like.

The Sussex chicken is an English breed and was once the most common for meat across Britain. They have brown plumes with white specks. This unique pattern is pretty to look at but it also serves as camouflage in the wild.

New Hampshire Red Chickens

New Hampshire Reds are more commonly chosen for meat than egg purposes but they also make a good dual-purpose bird.

Their early maturity means you can choose birds to use as meat more frequently.

These are descendants of Rhode Island Red chickens. They have a wide range of personalities, with some being more aggressive and being focused on the pecking order and others being more relaxed. They are a good choice for someone who is frequently keeping a watchful eye on their chickens. Otherwise, you may want a more docile breed.

Brahma Chickens

Brahma chickens are popular for their calm nature. Those birds are quite large, they are also quite docile.

They are a good choice among chicken farmers in the north, as the hardiness and large size of these chickens makes them a good choice in damp or cold climates. Part of this is due to their feathered feet, which keep them warm.

Brahma birds were originally developed for meat production, as they only lay an average of 150 brown eggs each year. However, their personality makes them an excellent choice as a pet.

Jersey Giant Chickens

As the name suggests, these chickens are quite large. These are dual-purpose birds, laying around 260 brown eggs each year. Their giant size comes along with a calm, tame personality that makes them perfect as a beginner chicken. Jersey Giant chickens are the biggest bird of the pure breeds and they come in white, black, and blue varieties.

Wyandotte Chickens

Also known as American Sebright chickens, these pretty birds are known for laying large quantities of eggs while remaining good meat birds.

Wyandotte's chickens lay brown eggs and thrive in a wide range of weather conditions. They also have docile personalities and striking coats. The most common birds of this variety have silver-laced feathers.

Plymouth Rock Chickens

This attractive breed's most common variety is the Barred Rock chicken, which has black and white stripes.

These birds are native to Massachusetts and are another dual-purpose bird. Their wide range of purposes, attractiveness, and gentle personality once made the Plymouth Rock chicken the most common breed across America. Other varieties include White Buff, Partridge, Columbian, Black, Blue, Penciled, and Silver.

The Plymouth Rock bird is friendly and can do well when confined, however, they will be happier with a chance to roam freely. You'll have to be careful about overheating in warm climates.

Australorp Chickens

This dual-purpose chicken can lay up to 250 brown eggs for the year. Native to Australia, these chickens come in varieties of white, black, and blue.

They have friendly personalities and are docile birds. Another benefit is their ability to forage, which allows them to hunt for treats and insects on the ground around their coop.

There are plenty of options when it comes to choosing a chicken breed. So, how do you go about adding birds to your flock? The best thing you can do is conduct the proper research—this is the only foolproof way to be sure you know what you are getting yourself into. It can be easy to get attracted to a bird for its appearance or personality.

Before long, you may find yourself stopping at farms or livestock shows in the hopes of adding to your flock.

What is Your Purpose for Raising Chickens?

The first thing you should consider is what you expect from your chickens. Do you want nutritious eggs all-year-round or are you trying to raise chickens for meat? Do you want to do a little bit of both? Is your main purpose related to foods or are you going to look at your chickens as a pet? Are you interested in breeding?

Some chickens are better adapted to being used as meat, while others have high egg-laying capacities that make them a good egg-laying bird.

If you plan on using your chickens for eggs and meat, you'll want to look for a dual-purpose bird or have a variety of chicken breeds. Some good egg-laying birds include Leghorn, Plymouth Rock, Australorp, Rhode Island Red, and Buff Orpington chickens. These breeds lay an egg almost every day.

The best meat birds are those that are large and grow to full size quickly. Some popular choices include Jersey Giant and Cornish Cross birds.

Dual-purpose breeds are large enough to provide meat but also frequently lay eggs. Some popular choices include Australorp and Buff Orpington chickens.

For breeding, you'll want to choose a broody breed, especially if you do not have money for an incubator. Broody birds are birds that make good mothers, as they do not mind sitting on eggs and will raise chickens.

Pekins, Buff Orpingtons, Australorps, and Silkies are all good broody birds. Some people choose to buy birds for show, as they would showcase a prized dog. You might find that you pay hundreds of dollars or more for a show chicken. However, you might find less expensive breeds.

Does Egg Color Matter?

Many people are surprised to find there is a greater variety than just white or brown eggs. Eggs come in all shades of brown, including dark brown, cream, and with spots.

There are also a wide variety of green eggs, from olive green to pastel green to sage green. Other colors include various shades of pink and blue. Here's a breakdown of some chicken varieties and the color of eggs that they lay:

- White- Polish, Hamburg, Lakenvelder, Leghorn, Ancona, Andalusian

- Pink/Cream- Easter Egger, Java, Faverolles, Orpington, Australorp, Sussex, Silkie

- Blue- Ameraucana, Easter Egger, Cream Legbar, Araucana

- Dark Brown- Marans, Welsummer, Penedesenca, Barnevelder

- Green- Easter Egger, Favaucana, Olive Egger

How Much Space Do You Have?

Not everyone has limitless acres to let their chickens roam on, especially if they live in the city. You may also be limited by the size of your yard.

While you can average that each chicken will need about three square feet of space in their coop, keep in mind that larger or more active breeds will need more room.

You do not have to allow your chickens to roam freely, especially if you are worried about them running into the road or being attacked by local predators. Chicken runs are another option—but keep in mind that these can get really expensive.

As you consider size, you'll also need to think about how many chickens you'll have. If there is not enough space, your chickens are more likely to fight amongst themselves.

They'll also be more susceptible to disease and you'll find the coop gets dirty a lot faster. If you are limited on space, Bantams are generally a good choice because of their small size and calm nature.

How is the Weather in Your Area?

Your overall climate is going to affect which birds will be most comfortable in your area. The various chicken species have evolved over time and adapted to their unique climate.

Some are larger and have a heavy coat of feathers, while other breeds are better suited to warmer climates.

While you can take precautions to keep your chickens cool in the summer and warm in the winter, it is better to choose birds adapted to the weather in your area. This will help them keep regular when laying eggs as well.

Sam Norton

Chapter 2.
How to Raise Chickens
without Land

The term "chicken coop" has different meanings to different people. In this booklet, the "coop" is the structure where chickens go to spend the night. In addition to this coop, they will have some kind of outdoor run area, whether this is free range or enclosed. Some people mix these two areas together and call them both a "coop". To keep things clear, I will refer to the inside area as the "coop" and the outside area as the "run".

Happy chickens lay lots of eggs, so it is in your basic self-interest to keep them happy. Happy chickens need a minimum of four (4) square feet of coop space per bird, plus a run area of at least ten (10) square feet per bird. I base these numbers on the recommendations of Gail Damerow in Storey's Guide to Raising Chickens

If there is no outside run area, then chickens need ten (10) square feet of coop space per bird. I will ignore this last suggestion, because you should not be keeping chickens if you cannot provide them with some outside space to move around in (whether this space is free range or in an enclosed pen). So let's look at the first number: four (4) square feet of coop space per bird.

If your chickens are outside most of the time, basically using the coop just for sleeping and laying eggs, then four (4) square feet per bird is adequate. If chickens are kept in the coop for long periods when they cannot go outside, especially if you are trying to over winter them inside, then they need extra coop space. The proper coop size also depends on the size of the chickens you are keeping. Bantams are much smaller than standard birds, so you can fit more of them in any given coop.

Even for standard birds, there is a big difference between an eight pound Orpington and a five pound Ameracauna hen. For medium-sized breeds like Ameracauna, I would feel more comfortable using the minimum size, while a flock of larger birds like Orpys could get pretty crowded with only four (4) square feet per bird. Tight conditions make for more fighting and risk of disease, so give them plenty of space.

Let's apply the four (4) square foot recommendation in the small backyard setting. Two hens would need a coop of at least eight (8) square feet, say two feet by four feet (2' x 4'). Three hens would need twelve (12) square feet, which might be a three by four foot (3' x 4') coop. Four hens would need sixteen (16) square feet, which could be accomplished with either a four by four (4' x 4') square coop or a more rectangular three and a half by five (3.5' x 5'). This should not seem like a lot of space, since it is only a few inches larger than a standard-sized bathtub.

But the outdoor run area will take up the most space. The run area should provide at least ten (10) square feet of space for each chicken. Again, this is a minimum, which I would increase by a few feet if the feeder and waterer take up part of the space. So let's crack the numbers again to see how this looks for a city dweller with a small backyard. Two hens would need a run space of at least twenty (20) square feet, perhaps three and a half feet by six feet (3.5' x 6'). Three hens would need thirty (30) square feet, either in a block of around five by six feet (5' x 6') or a strip such as three by ten feet (3' x 10'). Four hens would need forty (40) square feet, which you could create with a five by eight foot (5' x 8') block or a four by ten foot (4' x 10') plot.

Do not ignore side yards as possible run areas. At my daughter's former school, which has two hens we donated, they keep the chickens in a coop attached to a long, narrow fenced strip next to the building. This pen, which the children can walk inside to play with the chickens and harvest eggs, is only about three feet wide, but at least 20 feet long. It could have been used as a long flower bed at one time.

At only three feet wide, I may never have seriously considered this for a chicken area, but it provides these two hens with plenty of run space. There are some shelves and an old rabbit hutch on one end, which were turned into an open-sided coop. The coop is covered from the rain and the climate is quite mild, so the chickens do not complain that it is only enclosed on only three sides. Their wild ancestors slept in trees, not small houses.

The run space does not need to be square or rectangular, though that is usually the easiest way to go. In the run area, make sure to have some perches they can roost on during the day; I use one-inch thick dowels or garden stakes, placed 2-3 feet off the ground.

The main concern with the run is to keep it covered with plenty of mulch or bedding. Chicken manure makes the soil toxic very quickly, but this can be balanced (and odors nearly eliminated) with the addition of some carbon-rich mulch/bedding.

A thick layer of straw, leaves, shredded paper, or sawdust as bedding will help the chicken manure decompose naturally and create balanced compost. Keep at least a few inches of this mulch on the ground at all times, and change it every couple of months. Old chicken bedding with manure can go right into a compost bin or tumbler, where it will decompose and make a rich addition to your garden soil the next year.

My chickens have a fully enclosed run which is a little larger than this minimum size. I built this enclosure with a frame of 1 ½ x 1 ½ inch wooden stakes, covered with half inch wire mesh that is secured by large staples. Part of the run is shaded by the coop, which sits on top of it, providing some protection from the elements on hot or rainy days.

Even the bottom of the run is lined with poultry wire, though the soil and mulch on top of it are deep enough that the chickens never scratch down to the wire.

The coop is open to the run, so that the chickens can use it every day. If I am away from home, this is where they spend the day. I do not need to close anything up at night because the coop and run are sealed. Predators and pests (such as raccoons and rats) cannot get in.

When I am home, there is a gate I can open to give them more outdoor space. Attached to the gate is an extended run area behind my raised vegetable beds and under some fruit trees. It is lined with temporary plastic fences to keep the chickens out of my vegetable garden, and since I do not consider these fences very strong, I only let the chickens out into this area when I am home (which may only be an hour or two in the morning or evening).

These fences, in turn, are attached to a third run area, which is made from a couple of temporary dog fences. I move this around, sometimes letting them into part of the yard to eat weeds and bugs, and other times directing them onto one of my raised beds, which they can scratch in for a few months at a time. They aerate and fertilize the soil, which I often cover with compost or mulch that they dig in for me.

Here is a picture of them doing their thing in part of a raised bed, which has a movable, temporary fence protecting the vegetables and blueberries.

The chickens love to take dust baths in this deep soil also, which is an important part of their hygiene and pest protection. A months or two after letting them into the bed, they will have it thoroughly transformed (though I cannot plant in the soil until their manure breaks down a bit, say 6-12 months, since the ammonia needs to convert to plant-usable nitrogen).

After a hawk dropped in one day and tried to attack a full-sized hen, I covered the extended run with plastic bird netting. Putting this on only took a few minutes because it does not need to be secured too well; the mere sight of it seems to keep chickens in and hawks out.

Chapter 3.
Taking Care for Your Chicken Flock

We are normally conscious about having a decent immune system in every creature that we are concerned about even us humans.

A healthy immune system even in people is very important; essentially the component wards off ailment, illness, and contamination. That is a tremendous activity since small scale life forms are always surrounding us and our chickens!

All together for a chicken to successfully have a healthy immune system they must be fit and have every one of the things it should be in a harmonious situation.

Those factors that lead to a healthy immune system are nutrients, minerals, great nourishment, low stressors and adequate rest.

There is no convenient solution or a single thing that will fix everything – be incredulous of such cases. Your herd needs numerous things to help in having a healthy immune system.

Numerous different things administer the invulnerable reaction additionally – hereditary components, age, gut wellbeing, incendiary conditions or poor condition. A portion of those things we can't change, yet we can positively help with great, gainful sustenance and enhancements.

This season is an extraordinary time to check every hen for any medical issues and treat as needs are.

Guaranteeing your young chickens have a low-pressure condition is vital, so endeavor to keep things smooth and routine around the coop.

Chickens are pretty sensitive to changes, anything new can be unpleasant for them – except if it's palatable!

Rest as well, is very important. During this season it might appear as though everything they do is eat or rest, however that is alright.

They have a bustling year in front of them when the egg laying and chick raising season begins up, those hens will have the bounty to do and it will negatively affect their bodies.

Immune Booster 1: Garlic

Garlic is amazing food to a healthy immune system. It is likewise an antimicrobial, repulses parasites and is said to dissuade intestinal worms all while animating the invulnerable immune system.

You can include 4 cloves of pounded garlic to a gallon of drinking water.

On the off chance that your winged creatures aren't utilized to garlic, ensure they are drinking enough water – include another consumer of customary water if necessary. Try not to utilize garlic in a metal consumer – garlic will erode it.

You should change out the cloves every 2-3 days and supplant with crisp cloves. You can likewise utilize crisp garlic powder on the off chance that you have it available.

Similarly, as with most things, an excessive amount of can is a terrible thing – garlic can cause Heinz pallor which causes shortcoming in chickens.

Immune Booster 2: Herbs

There are numerous herbs that are prescribed to help in chickens wellbeing and absorption. Truth be told, some business chicken concerns have begun adding oregano and cinnamon oil to their feathered creatures' eating regimen.

Oregano – is the most loved for a restorative lift? It is said to support the resistant framework and gatekeepers against specific contaminations, for example, salmonella, irresistible bronchitis, avian flu, and E. coli.

Cinnamon – is an extraordinary all-rounder. It has antibacterial properties, lessens aggravation and is a cancer prevention agent.

Turmeric – has extraordinary anti-infection and against infective advantages.

Ginger – is another enemy of infective, against viral herb that helps the resistant framework.

Parsley – oozing with nutrients A, B, C, E, and K in addition to various follow components, it is said to invigorate egg laying.

The rundown can be broad yet these herbs above are the most well-known.

In spite of the fact that chickens don't have an incredible feeling of smell, they do have one. So sprinkling crisp herbs, for example, lavender in the coop and particularly the home boxes may place them in a quiet and glad temper.

There are numerous natural products that are solid for your chicken: melons, watermelons, grapes, bananas, and berries being the most every now and again advertised.

A citrus natural product is one of those things that the jury hasn't settled on. Numerous people say their group cherishes citrus (not lemons) but then others will disclose to you it's awful for them however no subtleties on what occur in the event that they eat it.

Here is a portion of the organic products you can nourish your chickens to support their immune system:

Bananas – contain nutrients B6 and B12, in addition to magnesium, potassium, fiber, and protein. On the off chance that likes me you don't care for eating wounded bananas, the young chickens will enable you to out!

Blueberries – Berries also are pressed brimming with stimulating supplements. Nutrients and following components, for example, selenium and phosphorus flourish.

They help in assimilation and contain cell reinforcements. I want to watch the young chickens race after solidified blueberries... it gives them to practice as well.

Strawberries – another superfood for your chickens. Brimming with nutrients, minerals, cell reinforcements and is a ground-breaking invulnerable promoter, it will surely nourish the young chickens too!

Raspberries, blackberries – all are delighted in by the hens. On the off chance that you have a thorn fix, you will locate a couple of valiant hens in there eating every one of the berries they can discover.

Make a point to likewise peruse what not to nourish your chickens.

Immune Booster 3: Greens

New green veggies pack heaps of nutrients and goodness. For instance – kale contains nutrients A, C, K, B6 in addition to calcium, potassium, copper, and manganese.

Your hens will appreciate some new greens as a treat and it doesn't need to be the 'customary' costly grocery store greens; think dandelions, chickweed, and plantain.

Turn the chickens out to unfenced and they will set out straight toward the grass and peck away joyfully.

Dandelions – contain nutrients A, B, C, E and K and various follow components, for example, calcium and manganese. It is said to help assimilation; it is a cancer prevention agent and furthermore a calming torment reliever.

Plantain – another firm most loved with energizing advantages. It contains nutrients and minerals and the seeds are said to be a characteristic wormer and detoxifier.

You can likewise make a recuperating ointment from plantain – there are a few formulas out there on the web. Other basic weeds that are advantageous to your chickens are clover, chickweed, and wild strawberries. Obviously, this is only a little inspecting of the decency accessible for nothing, directly under their mouths!

Immune Booster 4: Tonics

The most effortless and least expensive 'tonic' for your chickens is apple juice vinegar.

It is extraordinary for the processing and expands calcium retention particularly in the mid-year months – it is likewise somewhat clean. The suggested portion is 1 tablespoon/1 gallon water. Try not to use in metal compartments, it will make them erode as it is acidic.

There are likewise various businesses 'tonics' and enhancements out there too that are helpful to your herd.

Immune Booster 5: Seeds and Grains

Aged feed for your chicken is a brilliant method to help their nourishment in the desolate winter months.

Feed that has been matured is higher in nutrients B, C and K contain probiotics which help to process and expands the accessibility of the supplements that were bolted inside the grain.

This technique for bolstering diminishes feed utilization and waste all while boosting the insusceptible framework!

Another fast and fortifying thought for your fowls is grown seeds. Seeds are in all respects astutely made. They keep a considerable lot of the supplements bolted inside and when gobbled don't surrender them. To open the seeds internal goodness, you can absorb the seeds water until they begin to grow – they are then prepared for the young chickens to eat.

On an instance that you make that one stride further and let the seeds develop, you have grub for your young chickens.

Offer corn to the young chickens in the prior night sleep time else they will top off on this rather than the more nutritious feed. This will keep their stomach related tract occupied during that time hours.

Immune Booster 6: Eggs and Dairy

Eggs! They are beneficial for you and they are useful for the chickens as well! As a treat on cool days, blend them up some fried eggs – you can add your dried herbs to the blend as well.

Chickens don't process milk items well by any means, however, you can give little measures of yogurt to them added to maybe some oats or feed crush on a particularly cool day. My most loved pound is warm oats with some additional birdseed, oregano and 2-3 extensive spots of yogurt. Combine everything and stand well back before they begin throwing oats all over the place!

Remember to give them the eggshells as well. Prepare the shells in the stove on a low temperature for around an hour and ensure the shells are pulverized down into little, minor pieces so they aren't conspicuous as eggshells – you don't need them eating their own new eggs!

Giving them back the eggshells encourages them to get more calcium into their bodies prepared for the laying season.

Sam Norton

Chapter 4.
Best Egg Laying Chicken Breed

B ear in mind that the ideas below are ideal for people with little experience looking for easy-to-handle backyard chickens, needing little upkeep and, most importantly, laying a lot of eggs!

Rhode Island

Red Rhode Island Reds are associated with chicken keeping in the backyard and one of the most common chicken breeds in the country. They're friendly, easy to keep, and very tough.

Eggs: should produce more than 250 medium-sized brown eggs per year.

Character: It's very easy to keep, it doesn't take too much room and it's all year round.

Character: Hybrids tend to make excellent surfaces, eat less meat, and are not likely to be broody. We make a great selection, just make sure you get your cross from a responsible breeder and make sure it's not over-bred.

Buff Orpington

Buff Orpington is one of the simplest and most common egg laying chickens in the world. They reside from Kent, England, and are known for their good looks and sturdiness.

Eggs: should be produced at least 180 medium-sized, light brown eggs per year.

Character: A very friendly bird that performs best as a free-range and makes a perfect backyard hen.

They're also extremely friendly to people, so good if you want to teach them to feed from your side!

Leghorn

The leghorn breed originates from Italy and was first imported to the USA in the 1800s. They don't get broody sometimes, and they're the perfect choice for year round egg laying.

Eggs: should produce more than 250 medium-sized white eggs per year.

Character: Leghorns will be great in the gardens as they are a very healthy bird, but they are not very tame so they are not ideal for people with children who want them as a shelter.

Pick a breed and start with it. This will help to reduce pests and stop them from attacking each other.

Chickens is typically bred for meat or eggs, and each chicken farm must decide its business intent—raising eggs, growing chickens for the meat industry and providing a mixed farm, with both eggs laid chickens and chickens more appropriate for meat processing.

As far as the most competitive egg laying chickens are concerned, these are the best chicken breeds for this reason.

Australorp chickens are very healthy, with a rapid growth speed, beginning to lay eggs in the 5th month.

They are ideal for growing in an enclosed environment, but provide better egg production if they can walk freely in the open space.

Such chickens are not good at flying, making it possible to expand in an open space, not having a large shelter.

The hens of this breed are quite resilient, quickly going through cold winters, without impacting their egg laying speed.

Lohmann Brown Classic chicken breed

It is the most common breed of laying chicken in the world and is used in almost every part of the world. The Lohmann breed has a small size, with a body weight not exceeding 2 kilograms. A chicken of this breed produces up to 313 eggs per year, with a low feed consumption of just 110 grams per day.

Rhode Island Red chicken breed

The breed originated in the USA, where it is used for a dual purpose, both for eggs and meat. Such chickens are most common with small chicken farmers because they can easily adapt to backyard environments, have a high resistance to disease, and typically have a rather rough temperament. Rhode Island Red chicken can lay up to 260 eggs a year.

Marans chicken breed

It's a chicken breed native to France, with a very rich and colorful plumage. It has an annual production of 180-220 eggs and can be produced for both meat and eggs. The average egg is 60 grams and the shell is brown.

Having chickens that can regularly produce plenty of eggs is of great benefit and a highly sought-after attribute for most chicken farmers.

And if this is going to be your primary purpose for having chickens there are a few types of birds in particular that can help you maximize your results. It is usually breeds that are known as "hybrid hens" that lay the most eggs. Among these, the most widely used hybrid is one humorously called the, "Golden Comet".

These breeds can produce a large volume of eggs without having to consume too much chicken feed in the process.

These birds can typically produce about 280 eggs every single year. As their name might imply, the "Golden Comet" is usually yellow, or gold in color, with fluffy feathers. If you need a chicken to make you some eggs, be on the lookout for this birdie.

If your primary motive is to have great deals of eggs, you should select a type that is effective. Some top alternatives consist of Leghorn, Rhode Island Red, Black Australorp, Buff Orpington, as well as Sussex.

If you are getting hens to provide a numerous supply of eggs for your household after that, you need to see to it that your egg supply can stay on par with demand.

Respected layers like the Gingernut Ranger can provide you with as much as 7 eggs a week, so take that into account when determining the number of chickens you will certainly require. A few of these types will certainly ruin one egg a day.

Keep in mind that chickens will undergo a down season annually and quit lying or lay, so it will yield lesser than usual for a duration of time. If you are raising chickens largely for their eggs, be sure to pick a type with great to exceptional egg manufacturing.

Good egg production ranges from 125 to 175 eggs per year, per chicken — excellent manufacturing varies from 150 to 200 eggs per year, per hen. Outstanding manufacturing exceeds 230 eggs per year and some can yield as much as 300 eggs a year under the appropriate conditions.

While this is a small consideration, if egg dimension or shade is important to you, you'll intend to pick your chicken type as is necessary.

Generally, smaller sized breeds produce smaller eggs, so if you want huge eggs, try to find bigger, heavier types.

If you are in search of egg-layers, the black, red, and gold Sexlink breeds are excellent choices. The Black Sexlink is a cross between the Rhode Island Red rooster and the Barred Rock hen. It is generally docile and lays about two hundred and forty large brown eggs per year.

The Red Sexlink is a cross between the Rhode Island Red rooster and the Rhode Island White hen. It typically lays about two hundred and forty large brown eggs per year. The Gold Sexlink, on the other hand, is a well-known hybrid chicken that lays about two hundred and fifty large brown eggs per year.

The California White and the California Gray breeds are good choices too. Both of them can lay about three hundred large white eggs per year. In addition, you can choose Black Star hens.

They are a cross between the Rhode Island Red rooster and the Barred Rock hen. They produce above average amounts of large brown eggs. Crested Cream Legbars are also ideal.

They can lay up to one hundred and eighty medium blue or bluish-green eggs. If you want a really high amount of eggs, you should choose the Goldline. This hybrid can lay up to three hundred and twenty large brown eggs per year.

You can also choose to raise Marans since they can lay a good number of medium to large dark brown eggs.

The Copper Black Marans can actually lay up to two hundred eggs per year. Other great hybrids you can choose are Nera, Amber, and Speckledly. The Nera is a cross between the Rhode Island Red rooster and the Barred Plymouth Rock hen. It can lay around two hundred and seventy eggs per year.

The Amber, on the other hand, can lay up to three hundred medium eggs per year. Finally, the Speckledly, which is a cross between the Rhode Island Red rooster and the Maran, can lay around two hundred and seventy large dark brown eggs per year.

Sam Norton

Chapter 5.
Planning and Buying Your Chickens

T here are many important decisions you need to make before becoming a chicken owner. Once you have made this decision, it is time to move onto the next important decisions.

You will learn how to purchase your flock, what to look for, whether to buy chicks or chickens, male or female chickens, and the essentials of flock planning.

Eggs, Chicks, or Adult Birds?

There are three ways in which you can start raising chickens and it is for you to decide which of the following best suits your needs. For the absolute beginner, I would recommend starting with chicks: not only is it the most economical and practical way to start raising chickens, but seeing chicks grow to be adults is also a fascinating journey.

Starting with Fertile Eggs

There are several reasons why you may choose to hatch your own eggs instead of purchasing chicks or adult birds.

Watching eggs hatch is an exciting and beautiful experience. You get to really connect with the life cycle of your chickens and you also get the opportunity to hatch rare breads and unusual colors.

Before purchasing fertile eggs of rare breeds however, it is advised to first practice your incubation technique. Incubation is tricky even with the best incubation equipment and you should never expect more than 50% of your eggs to hatch.

Lastly, it is important to keep in mind that you will have roosters in your flock if you decide to hatch eggs yourself. Eggs will usually hatch out in a 50:50 ratio of males and females.

If you live in an urban setting, having roosters may be problematic: they are significantly louder than hens and keeping them is often against municipal regulations.

Hatching and incubation is a skill in itself. However, for beginners and those who don't want to invest in additional equipment for hatching and incubation, it is recommended that you start with either baby chicks or adult birds.

Male or Female Chickens?

Whether you need hens, roosters, or both will depend on your chicken-raising goals. If you are raising chickens that lay eggs, purchase either adult hens or female pullets (young hens) that have been sexed. Adult hens are more expensive but it will save you the waiting time.

If your primary aim of keeping chicken is for meat, it is advised to order only cockerels (young males).

Cockerels grow larger and faster than pullets and you generally won't have any problems with fighting unless you wait too long to butcher them.

It is important to keep in mind that hens do not need a rooster around to lay eggs and to live a normal life. If you live rurally and are not interested in breeding chickens, it might be a good idea to not keep a crowing rooster.

Furthermore, if you intend to keep a small number of backyard chickens, it is not advised to have a rooster at all.

For every rooster, there should be around 10 – 12 hens in your flock. If you do decide to keep roosters, there are a few considerations to be made: Make sure to choose the right breed for your backyard rooster. The breed will determine your rooster's temperament.

The favorite breeds for roosters and multiple roosters include Brahmas, Orpingtons, Silkies (ornamental birds), Plymouth Rocks, Marans, and Australorps.

Make sure that you have a plenty of running space and a couple of safe places to separate someone from the flock if necessary.

If you plan to keep multiple roosters, it is advisable to raise them together in your flock. This way, they will establish a natural pecking order between them as them grow up which will ensure peace in your backyard!

How Many?

It is important to note that chickens are social creatures and therefore it's crucial that you purchase at least two chickens to keep them happy.

How many chickens you can ultimately raise will depend on your space, the size of your chicken coop, as well as local rules and regulations that sometimes limit the amount of chickens you can keep.

When deciding on how many chickens to keep, there are two primary considerations: space and eggs. The number of birds you wish to keep will also depend on your needs. If you have chosen chickens from a good laying breed, you can expect to receive 5-6 eggs per week. If your hens are not from an egg-laying strain, you can still expect to receive 2-3 eggs per week per hen. The size of your chicken coop will also determine the size of the flock you can keep.

There should be around 2 to 4 sq. feet of floor area in your coop for each, and at least 4 sq. feet of area in the outdoor run.

Purchasing and Starting with Chicks

As mentioned earlier, starting your chicken-raising experience with baby chicks is the most economical and practical way, especially if you are a beginner. There are many reasons for this, which include the following:

- Most hatcheries will see the chicks for you.
- Chicks are usually less expensive than adult birds.
- Chicks are less likely to carry parasites or disease compared to adult birds.

Despite this, there are certain disadvantages to starting with baby chicks. Chicks are fragile and need protection. They require a lot of attention and special brooding equipment to keep them warm and protected. They also need time to mature and it will take at least 5 months or sometimes longer before female chicks mature to a stage where they start laying eggs.

On top of this, it is important to keep in mind that the younger the chick, the harder it is to determine sex. While some hatcheries do a pretty good job in sexing chicks, mistakes do sometimes occur.

It is also difficult to judge the quality of newly hatched chicks and you are therefore left with some ambiguity in terms of the sex as well as the quality of your chick.

You will also find that some hatcheries will offer 'starter birds'. These are older birds that are easier to sex, take less time to mature, and you will also have a better idea as to their quality.

The cost of shipping starter birds is usually greater as they require special handling and it is also important to bear in mind that your choice in terms of breed selection will be more limited with starter birds. If you do opt for starter birds, make sure to find out their age as this will determine whether or not you will need a breeder.

The easiest time to purchase baby chicks is in the spring and the early summer. You can purchase chicks either through online hatcheries or from farm stores or local breeders.

Purchasing Mail-Order Chicks

The following is a list of to-dos and things to be aware of when purchasing mail-order chicks:

When ordering chicks online, there is usually a minimum order of 25 chicks. This is because chicks need to be packed closely together in boxes to keep them warm during shipping.

Try to order your chicks when the weather is mild in your area. This is because even though they are grouped together; baby chicks can overheat or become too cold during transit.

Mail-order chicks are usually hatched on demand. This means that when you order your chicks, they will first stay in the incubator for around 21 days before they are shipped out to you.

Baby chicks can survive for 2-3 days without food or water after hatching. Baby chicks are usually shipped the day after they hatch and usually reach you within 24 hours (by U.S. Mail).

When choosing an online hatchery, try and choose one that does guarantee 24-hour delivery to your area. To ensure a happy arrival, it is best to keep the shipping time as short as possible.

Do not order any extras – hatcheries will usually add one or two free chicks to cover any possible losses during shipping. Some hatcheries will guarantee safe arrival while others do not.

When your chicks get delivered or when you go to the post office to collect them (this will depend on the hatcheries' courier), make sure to open the box and inspect them immediately.

In the event that you have lost some chicks, make sure to inform the post office. If your hatchery guarantees safe arrival, you can fill out a claims form and receive a refund or a replacement. Make sure to count your chicks before filing a claim as some hatcheries will add extra chicks to your order to account for any possible losses.

From a Local Breeder

Depending on where you live, you might also have the opportunity to purchase chicks from a local breeder. There are advantages and disadvantages of acquiring your chicks this way.

Visiting your local breeder is usually an exciting and fun experience and you also get to speak to them directly to get some help and advice. You can build a relationship with your chicks straight away and you will also get a chance to see whether they look healthy and happy, which is a key advantage.

On the other hand, breeders will rarely be able to vaccinate chicks against diseases. Furthermore, chick sexing is a specialist skill – it is possible that your local breeder won't be able to tell you what sex the chicks are.

From a Farm Store

You may also be able to purchase some chicks from a local farm store. Some farm stores take orders and some will only sell chicks in the spring. A great upside is that you can usually order less than 25 which is ideal for those with a small backyard coop.

Some farm stores will also have some chicks to be bought on the spot. Ask around to see whether anyone knows what breed or sex the chicks are. If you are unsure about the information you receive, ask the person exactly how they know what sex the chick is. Bear in mind that it is impossible to tell what sex a newly hatched chick is by simply looking at it.

You can only know the sex of a newly hatched chick if the chick is from a sex-linked line. If the store has just bought mixed chicks, be cautious as there is a chance that they are all roosters, or not the type or breed of chicken that you are after.

Sam Norton

Chapter 6.
Providing Food and Water

Chickens are good feeders. They will eat almost everything offered to them. As such, there is not really a right way to feed them especially backyard chickens. Commercial chickens may need detailed feeding programs due to their huge numbers and controlling costs.

However, backyard chickens will get to feed on what is available. But since we want them to produce eggs for us constantly, we need to make sure we are feeding them something close to what they need. Just like any other animals, chickens will need a balanced diet and will also get fat when fed excessively.

The thing with knowing whether you are feeding your chickens right will be mostly through observation and trial and error.

Other variables such as the weather, stage of growth, activity levels, and type of breed will influence feeding.

So the information that I will provide here should only act as a guideline. The important thing is to understand your particular hens and behavior in order to note any changes that may require a feeding intervention.

The first thing to note is that the more area your chickens have, the less they'll rely on food from you. This is because they are able to forage and look for insects, small animals, worms and plant shoots to feed on.

As a matter of fact they love these more than anything else. These are nutritious for them and cannot cause any health problem. If your chickens are free rangers, you'll just need a little commercial feed for them to keep them well fed.

On the other hand, chickens that never leave the coop and fully depend on being feed need large quantities of food. If you fail to provide it, they might turn on each other or the wooden surfaces of the coop. Hungry hens are really angry hens. You'll also spend too much money which will beat your purpose of raising hens for eggs.

How to feed chicks

Chicks will normally depend on commercial feeds. This is because they are too young to forage themselves and they also need this early boost to develop properly.

The feeds will normally be called starter feeds. You can however feed them kitchen scraps at any stage.

Make sure you buy the right feed ex: starter feed for layers. However, if your chicks are broilers, or you are raising them for meat, buy their specific formulated feeds.

Feeding pullets

Pullets are teenage chickens between the ages of two months to five months. The main aim here is to get them strong and ready for their egg laying life.

They thus need to develop well and have strong bones.

Grower rations will make sure they do so and achieve normal body weight before they start laying eggs. At this age, they will be really active and will look for anything to eat.

If you allow them to forage, you'll need to limit their feeds. However provide plenty of water.

Laying hens

Laying hens are adult hens and their nutritional requirements drastically change. The eggs have a large component of calcium. This will be the most needed component in the feeds.

They have calcium reserves in the body but can easily get depleted. When this happens, the hen lays soft shelled eggs. If the depletion continues, they stop laying completely.

They are also likely to break their eggs and feed on the egg shell in search of calcium. A balanced layer feed should be provided daily.

You should also allow the hen to forage and look for insects and animals which are a vital source of protein. A calcium supplement would be good for them. Oyster shells provide high amounts of calcium and can be fed occasionally.

The eggs shells are also very high in calcium. You can feed them right back to the hen after you have eaten the contents inside. However, you need to crush these shells so that they are not recognizable. If your hen lays daily, do not limit the food as this is what she uses to make the eggs.

You should have a proper feeder that suits the amount of hens you have. This will limit any wastage which adds up the costs. Making your own feeder with 5 liter buckets or pop bottles can help save money as store bought feeders can be quite expensive.

A hens' instinct is to eat from the ground, which can cause their waste to get in the feed. Hanging the feeder can help prevent this and reduce waste since they will not be able to scratch out the feed.

Some feeders will allow you to stock up food that will last several days. This is important of you are out of the home for several days and nobody is available to feed the chickens.

Most chickens will just eat enough food, they have a good sense of self-regulation with only the exception of a few breeds and broilers.

This is especially true with adult laying hens, you need not worry that you are overfeeding them.

Feeding treats

Chickens like kitchen scraps. You'll notice that they'll follow you if they think you have something for them from the kitchen. Most of the foods we consume will be just fine for them.

However, moldy food might cause illness since it already has bacteria. Salty foods and sugary foods are also not good for your hens. Most of the kitchen scraps will be high energy foods that have lots of calories. It's good to feed these after you have served the commercial feeds. This will ensure that the hen doesn't overeat on them. All types of vegetable are good for your chickens.

They'll love them. You can hang them somewhere in the coop and let them peck at them whenever they fell like it.

Poultry feeds should be the main diet for your hens. Scraps and treats should serve as supplements to ensure that they are having a balanced diet.

If you have a large number of hens, you'll need to monitor them at feeding time to ensure that they are all eating. Hens are very social animals with clear social orders within a group. Dominant hens might exclude those lower in the order from feeding. If you notice this, you might need to provide more than one feeding point.

Always have clean drinking water available all the time. Find a good waterer that doesn't spill around the coop to reduce your cleaning work. A waterer that holds a large amount of water in a canister and only drips a little to the saucer will serve you well in case you are not at home.

Clean the waterer weekly as it can house germs. Beddings, scraps, dropping will also get in the saucer and need to be removed.

There are also many ways people make their own waterers with buckets, piping and pumps, this helps save on cost.

Water is essential for all living things, and chickens are no exception.

A hen drinks a cup of water every day. She's going to take frequent small sips all day. Too little water can impact egg production, among many other issues, so make sure they have plenty of water.

There's about 15 cups of water in one US gallon, so if you've got a lot of birds, you'll need a few drinkers for them.

Conclusion

S ince they are generally simple to keep up, chickens have for quite some time been the main decision for the vast majority endeavoring to raise their very own food.

A choice must be made right off the bat, and ideally before purchasing your flocks, regardless of whether you are going to utilize them for food, eggs, or both.

You should incorporate perches for evening time roosting, just as nesting boxes for them in case you plan on gathering eggs.

While picking the area for the chicken, try to take into account abundant grass zones too.

Offering simple access to clean nourishment and water is basic to their general wellbeing and you can find water dispensers at most feed stores. These are planned in view of neatness and sanitation. Contingent upon the sort of hens you will have, there are diverse style feeders to suit any exceptional needs.

The food utilized to feed them can be gotten at feed stores too, and can be picked to likewise suit the brood you procure.

Raising a chicken flock at home can be a good experience and a source of fun. This talks about living beings and accountability as a family project.

Whether you have little hens or bigger ones, they will require supplements just as the expansion of specific nutrients to help in creating more healthy eggs for human utilization. Grit helps in digestion, and squashed oyster shell enables their eggs to grow solid shells too. These products are generally accessible at feed stores too.

Selecting your hens is up to you, and since there is such a very huge measure of various assortments, the decisions are almost interminable.

A little research will go far in supporting you in your decisions, and teaching yourself on the best brooding hens, or best makers and so on, will likewise be of benefit to you when the opportunity arrives to select your breeds.

Prior to choosing whether you will have a rooster, it is basic that you think about all parts of having one. A rooster isn't vital for the hens to lay their eggs, but the eggs will essentially not be fertilized.

Anyway, they will keep on laying regardless of whether there is a rooster present. Remember that chickens are swaggering noisy animals, and can cause issues for you if you live in a relatively crowded or busy area. You don't have to have a major farming operation in order to enjoy the rewarding experience of raising chickens.

As long as you have a modest sized backyard, you too can reap the benefits that chickens provide. I hope that this book has enlightened you with plenty of tips and tricks to get started. Now it's just up to you, to bring the best of the farm, right to your backyard.

CPSIA information can be obtained
at www.ICGtesting.com
Printed in the USA
BVHW092057250621
610448BV00002B/315